YOUR KNOWLEDGE HAS VALUE

Bibliographic information published by the German National Library:

The German National Library lists this publication in the National Bibliography; detailed bibliographic data are available on the Internet at http://dnb.dnb.de .

Imprint:

Copyright © 2014 GRIN Verlag, Open Publishing GmbH
Print and binding: Books on Demand GmbH, Norderstedt Germany
ISBN: 978-3-668-03974-2

This book at GRIN:

http://www.grin.com/en/e-book/304560/technology-as-a-play-learning-tool-for-children-with-special-disabilities

Anna-Maria Papadopoulou

Technology as a play-learning tool for children with special disabilities. Literature review

GRIN Publishing

GRIN - Your knowledge has value

Since its foundation in 1998, GRIN has specialized in publishing academic texts by students, college teachers and other academics as e-book and printed book. The website www.grin.com is an ideal platform for presenting term papers, final papers, scientific essays, dissertations and specialist books.

Visit us on the internet:

http://www.grin.com/

http://www.facebook.com/grincom

http://www.twitter.com/grin_com

Technology as a play-learning tool for children with special disabilities : literature research review

Abstract

Purpose - The purpose of this study is to review and highlight existing research work in the field of computer assistive technology for children with multiple disabilities in educative play. Based on five major journals published between January 2002 and September 2011 related to computer based play in children with profound multiple disabilities, it sets out to describe internet use in assisting or enabling learning and social interaction.

Design/Methodology - The review was restricted to identification of the systems involved, identification of the experimental group, literature overview, ,identification of the type of psychological approach and conclusion.

Findings - Interactive computer play is a promising tool for assisting children with disabilities in aspects of social interaction, education and rehabilitation process but the level of evidence is limited at the time. Further and more research-based findings are needed.

Originality - This paper provides an original literature review by the author based on critical reviews of five major journals.

1. Introduction

Each year, a significant proportion of children who have or who will be at risk of having developmental disabilities are born. Such disabilities include down syndrome, sensory impairment, mental retardation, autism and brain inabilities. Children with multiple disabilities experience challenges in self care, education, social interaction, playing and learning problem-solving skills (Cavet, 1995).

Play is critical to the healthy grow and development of children. The benefits of play to one's physical health, problem solving, sociability and learning are evident. However, these benefits do not fulfill the demands of people with disabilities as pleasure is denied through commonly used ways of play leading to isolation (Global Vision Project, 2011). Research has shown that interactive computer technologies have led to multiple ways of educating and inducing positive results on cognitive function in children with sensory motor disorders (Sandlund, McDonough, Hager-Ross, 2008).

The most powerful indicator in the rapid change in society is the development of technology providing powerful means to access, transmit and interpret educative information using several subcategories (Hutiger 1994, Lesar 1998, Smedley et al 1997). The assistive type technology (AT) has been used as one strategy, especially in educational settings to enable children with disabilities to participate in numerous activities (Inge and Shepherd 1995, Derer et al 1996, Hutinger et al 1996, Margolis and Goodman 1999). A common tool that has been used through computer based play are pictures with specialized voice output which can deliver messages of self - confidence like "well done", "best score" and other related commands through digital clicks. However, more experimental techniques using virtual objects, creative play, writing, printing and software assistive technology have been tested showing positive results. Researchers described the absence of play experience that is caused by physical limitations as primary play deprivation and recognised the importance of studying the psychosocial impact of assistive technology (Cook et al. 2000; Day et al. 2002). Identifying the need to create technologies that enable children's acquisition of educational play experiences, researchers have exploited robotics and virtual reality environments (Davies, 1996; Cook et al., 2000, Miller and Reid, 2003 ;

Kronreif et al., 2005). Hawkins in 1976 discussed if and how the joy of discovery can stimulate children with severe multiple disabilities to become attentive. He stated that if children are offered an object that attracts them, they are in most cases spontaneously attentive, however this function has to be trained (Brodin, 1994) and research shows that there is a link between the level of activity and the cognitive activity.

As mentioned above the purpose of this study is to highlight information technology as a play-learning tool in children with profound multiple disabilities on a systematic four stage approach and focus on computer-based play as a dominant activity which is not discussed very often in research for children with disabilities and appears essential to child development (Brodin and Lindstrand 2003 , Sandberg 2003 , Retter 2003). A detailed description of the adopted methodology sets identification of the technology systems involved in play for children with cognitive disabilities, the experimental group used in each study, literature overview and the type of psychological approach. The psychological approaches are divided into four main groups, the biological, behaviourist , psychodynamic and cognitive approach.

2. Identification

In the process of examining the current research studies for technology as a play-learning tool for children with profound multiple disabilities, a number of technology systems were identified.

- A movement-to-music computer system was used, which gives children the ability to interact with the environment by producing valuable and enjoyable musical sounds for a therapeutic goal (Tam et al; 2007).
- Empirical study on 38 children using computers for play and training; tesing their preferences and prental views on children play. (Brodin; 2005).
- Interactive computer play (ICF) refers to any kind of computer game or virtual reality technique where a child can interact and play with virtual objects. ICF offers the physically disabled child an opportunity to be active and independent in activities in a safe environment that resembles real life (Miller S, Reid D, 2003).

- Review on video technology and persons with autism and other developmental disabilities (Sturmey P. 2003)
- Four developed systems were tested and divided into two categories; the educational applications and the entertainment applications (Savidis A; Grammenos D; Stephanidis C; 2007).
  - (a) Educational applications included an accessible "canteen manager" real-life application, training people with learning difficulties for the cashier management of a typical canteen and a multimedia "sewing tutorial" application on a personal computer training people with learning disabilities in typical sewing tasks.
  - (b) Entertainment applications included two accessible and very configurable action games for a combination of disabilities like hearing, motor, cognitive and vision impairments. The two action games were an accessible remake of the classic space invaders and the pong arcade games which proved to have a significant role in sharpening kinesthetic skills and decision making.

3. Literature overview

Learning disabilities is a term describing a number of dysfunctions such as dyslexia, dyscalculia, dysgraphia, dyspraxia, central auditory processing disorder, visual motor deficit and language disorders. A research has concentrated in developing an accessible application suite consisting of inclusive e-learning and e-entertainment applications, accommodating learning difficulties as well as motor , perception and coordination problems (Savidis A; Grammenos D; Stephanidis C; 2007). Overall, the paper discussed the development and evaluation of two inclusive training applications and two games for people with learning disabilities. Namely, the developed systems involved were : (a) a cashier training applications; (b) a sewing training applications; (c) an accesible pong game; and (d) an accessible action game. The main objective of researchers was to investigate the hypothesis that computer games computer games can have a significant role on improving the training of people with learning disabilities , such as Asperger syndrome. The results obtained from the task completion were extremely positive for first time use leading to practical working applications. The research effort was to establish a continuous informal educational process which can be smoothly integrated in daily activities within the friendly home environment. The developed applications were targeted to be effective in learning problems, also in combination with perception, fine motor or dexterity problems, through the development of accessible electronic training systems and through the combination of playing and training which makes the user experience more rewarding, pleasant and effective.An innovating electronic game is under development with co-operative group activities including social dynamics such as turn-taking and challenging skills such as critical thinking.

Tam , Schwellnus, Eaton, Hamdani, Lamont and Chau (2007) conducted a study to explore parent's experiences of using the movement-to-music computer system which allows children with limited movements to play and create music. Tam et al study was carried out using a qualitative method with in-depth interview techniques from the participants which were six mothers and their children. The themes extracted from the data were organized under two main concepts of the International Classification of Functioning (ICF) and disability and health (WHO,2001) framework. Results showed that the movement to music expanded horizons for the child along the ICF health dimensions and the MTM had a positive impact on the ICF environmental determinants of health. MTM has the potential to improve children's body functions and enhance their participation in family activities. Support previous research findings that participation in play promotes' children's physical , social and cognitive development. A limitation of the study was the small sample size that for future research it would be more necessary and valuable to use a larger sample in order to confirm findings.

In a research of Brodin J, in 2005, play in children with profound multiple disabilities is in focus. The aim of the study was to highlight studies on play as a tool for learning and early stimulation, and for training of different functions, as these aspects seem to be of great interest in research today. One reason for this might be the information and communication technologies that make it possible for children with profound disabilities to use computers for play and training and another reason is the diagnostic society where the diagnosis often is a prerequisite for receiving support from society (Linstrand, 1998; 2002). Brodin (2005) investigated the parental views on children's play as well as children's preferences on toys and play activities. The empirical study was conducted on 38 children with profound intellectual and multiple disabilities and their ages varied between 2,5 to 20 years old. The common findings in previous studies showed that among children with delayed development and deprived environments , that cognitive orientated programmes give the finest results (Broffenbrener, 1975). Based on these facts Nielsen (1988) developed assistive devices as well as a methodology for sensory stimulation of children and adults on an early developmental level. The results of Brodin J, empirical study showed that the parents experienced difficulties in activating their children in a meaningful way , that the children quickly lost their interest in objects and events, that they were passive and worried. Approximately 50% of the children in the study screened themselves off during play and this behavior affected the mothers' motivation to play and communicate with her child. From the results it appeared that the issue of being a parent of a child with profound multiple disabilities often needs great efforts from the parents. Some of the parents stated that they sometimes felt too tired to play with the child because the daily care takes them so much time that it was difficult to find time for playing with them.

In an attempt to examine systematically the evidence for the application of interactive computer play in the rehabilitation of children with sensory motor disorders; Sandlund M, McDonough S and Hager-Ross C in 2008 , carried out a review which was restricted to reports of intervention studies evaluating the impact of each factor. Researchers have defined interactive computer play (ICP) as any kind of computer game or virtual reality technique where the child can interact and play with virtual objects in a computer generated environment. Interactive computer technologies (ICP) were particularly appealing for use in the rehabilitation of children for the opportunity given to create fun and engaging environments that motivate the child to exercise (Schultheis, 2001). A total of 74 articles were identified, of which 16 met the inclusion criteria. The areas investigated in the systematic review based on three randomized controlled trials and case reports, were movement quality, spatial orientation and mobility, and motivational aspects. Two of the three randomized control trials investigating movement quality and one examining spatial orientation showed no significant improvements. Thirteen studies presented positive findings in the areas of movement quality, spatial orientation, mobility, motivation, playfulness and self-efficacy. A wide range of different outcome measures was used, for instance ten of the studies used valid and reliable outcome measures that were clearly described, six studies mainly used measures designed specifically for the study. ICD is a potentially promising tool for the motor rehabilitation of children but the level of evidence is too limited to assess its value fully, thus further convincing research is needed. None of the studies included in the review classified their research question in relation to the ICF dimensions of health or referred to the ICF in the discussion of measurements or results (Akhutina T, Foreman N, et al 2003).

The concept of video technology for persons with autism has been previously tested in imaginary play, teaching perspective and social interaction with peers. In a review contacted by Sturmey P (2003), the aim was to examine and state the potential of video technology within a broad package of positive behavioral support for children with disabilities. The author, expands the current review by addressing new behaviors such as perspective taking, independent, cooperative and imaginary play, academic skills and spontaneous requesting on four articles. Charlop-Christy and Daneshvar present an interesting study of the use of video technology in teaching perpsective taking to children with autism spectrum disorders. In their theory of mind, Baron-Cohen and Swettenham (1989) posited that children with autism have an inherent deficit in understanding the thoughts and feelings of others. They believed that these deficits reflect abnormalities in putative cognitive structures residing in as unknown yet regions of the brain. D'Atengo, Mangiapanello and Taylor adress how to increase imaginative play in a child with autistic disorder. They demonstrate that video modeling by an adult was effective at teaching a variety of imaginary play behaviors , such as having a tea party, to this child. There are two significant aspects in this study, firstly the child learned to engage in extended periods of pretend play without correction or reinforcement from another person and secondly, the child learned to do this by watching a 5-minute videotape one hour prior to the play session. This suggests that this technology has considerable applied potential. D'Ategno et al. suggest that imaginary play can be effectively taught using simple video modeling. Another important aspect of this study is the programming of nonsocial stimuli to promote appropriate behavior in children with autism (McClannaham, Krantz, 1997). Sturmey P. (2003) included another study by Kinney, Vedora and Stromer which reported on a novel application of video technology on teaching generative spelling to a child with autism using video modeling and video reinforcement. Wert and Neisworth present an evaluation of video self-monitoring to teach children with autistic disorder to self-initiate social interactions with peers. Their results indicated that video self-monitoring was very effective in increasing spontaneous requesting by all participants in their study. The four chosen articles demonstrate that video technology can be a powerful tool for teaching appropriate social behavior, academic tasks and independent play to autistic children. Concluding, Sturmey P. (2003) reviewed that further development of this technology is needed to effectively address perspective taking in all children with autistic disorders.

4. Experimental groups

The inclusive experimental groups used for the studies were mostly children with profound intellectual and multiple disabilities (Brodin J,2005; Sandlund et al,2008; Sturmey P,2003). Whereas in the study of Tam et al in 2007 , the experimental groups used were six mothers and their children who had special disabilities.

5. Type of psychological approach

There are various different approaches in existing psychology. An approach is a view that involves certain beliefs about the way humans function, what research methods are appropriate for each condition and which aspects of them are worth to study.

The cognitive perspective is concerned with functions such as perception, memory and attention. It views people as being similar to computers in the way we process information following a certain procedure. Cognitive Psychology revolves around the notion that if we want to know what makes people tick then we need to understand the internal processes of their mind. Cognition literally means "knowing" thus psychologists study cognition which is 'the mental act or process by which knowledge is acquired' (Neisser; 1967).

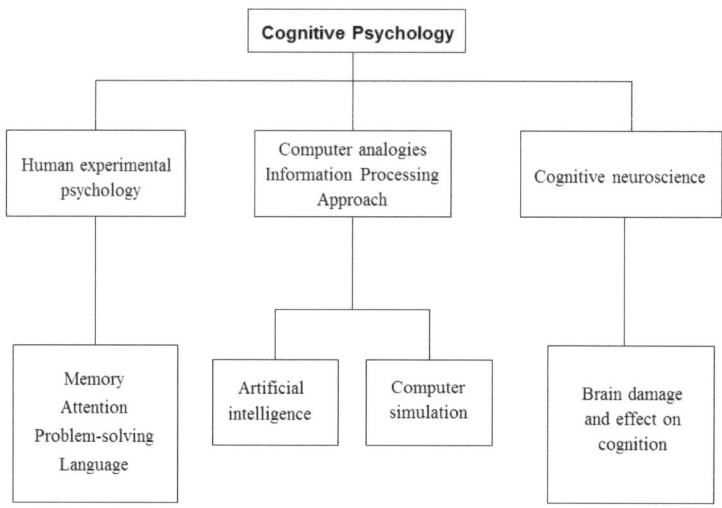

Children with learning disabilities grow up to be adults with learning disabilities. Research has shown that a set of individual characteristics, attitudes, and behaviors can help lead persons with learning disabilities to positive life outcomes. Unfortunately, we often concentrate our efforts primarily on educational areas, paying little attention to the development of these attributes in persons with learning disabilities which can be developed through play. Today's children are the first generation of the "digital age." They are being raised in a society that is changing rapidly as a result of the entry of computer-based technologies that provide more universal and faster worldwide links to commerce, communication, and culture (Glaser; 2000).

Technology as a play-learning tool for children with special disabilities concentrates mainly on cognition. In a study of Tam et al in 2007 results showed evidently that play is critically important to a child's development of cognitive, physical and psycho-social skills. Interactive computer technologies (ICP) were particularly appealing for the use in the rehabilitation of children for the opportunity given to create fun and engage in environments of exercise motivation via cognitive thinking (Sandlund; 2008).

Developing inclusive e-learning and e-entertainment applications lead to cognitive skills training as they have a positive effect on learning disabilities and encourage the access on IT systems (Savidis A; Grammenos D; Stephanidis C; 2007). Moreover, technology for children with special disabilities showed positive results on social behavior, independent play and noted as a powerful tool for critical thinking and academic tasks (Sturmey; 2003). Learning and early stimulation seem to be of a great interest today by contributing in the training of different functions (Brodin; 2005).

5. Conclusion

Interactive computer play for learning is a potentially promising tool for the motor rehabilitation and physical disability level of children with special needs. The range of target behaviors and different methods by which video technology was successfully used attests to its robustness as an approach for supporting appropriate behaviors in children with autism.

Although this literature review project concerns young children with profound multiple disabilities, the identified computer technology and materials can easily be adapted to older populations. Most importantly, the computer technology is non-contact which is essential to the children who have faced many invasive procedures in their rehabilitation.

Working together, teachers, parents and school members, as well as both students with disabilities and their non-disabled peers, can encourage the creation of technology friendly environments in which all students have equal opportunities to learn.

The obtained results of all the scientific research included in this paper are very positive and encouraging, and have led to the identification of new research directions, combining training and playing, through novel training techniques and purpose orientated games. There is no doubt that technology has the potential to act as an equalizer by freeing children from their special disability in a way that allows them to achieve true potential.

References

Jane Brodin (1999) Play in Children with Severe Multiple Disabilities:
Play with toys - a review, International Journal of Disability, Development and
Education,
46:1, 25-34

Jane Brodin (2010) Can ICT give children with disabilities equal opportunities in
school? Improving Schools vol. 13 no. 1 99-112

Brodin J. & Lindstrand P. (2003). What about ICT in special education? Special
educators evaluate information and communication technology as a learning tool.
European Journal of Special Needs Education 18 (1), 71-87.

Jane Brodin (2005) Diversity of aspects on play in children with profound multiple
disabilities, Early Child Development and Care, 175:7-8, 635-646.

Sandlund M, McDonough S, Hager-Ross C (2008). Interactive computer play in
rehabilitation of children with sensorimotor disorders: a systematic review. Health
and rehabilitation Sciences Research Institute.

Gillespie A, Best C, & O'Neill B, (2012). Cognitive function and assistive technology
for cognition : a review. Journal of the International Neuropsychological Society, 18,
1-19.

Peter Sturmey (2003). Video Technology and Persons with Autism and Other
Dvelopmental Disabilities : An Emerging Technology for PBS. City University of York,
Journal of positive behavior interventions , Volume 5, no.1, 3-4.

Tam C, Scwellnus H, Eaton C, Hamdani Y, Lamont A, & Chau T, (2007). Movement-to-
music computer technology: a developmental play experience for children with
severe physical disabilities. Occupational therapy intetrnational. Int 14(2):99-112.

A Savidis, D Grammenos, C Stephanidis - Universal Access in the Information Society,
2007. Developing inclusive e-learning and e-entertainment to effectively
accommodate learning difficulties. Universal access in the Information Society, Vol:5,
Issue 4, 401-419.

D. Kim Reid and Jan Weatherly Valle.(2004)The Discursive Practice of Learning
Disability : Implications for Instruction and Parent--School Relations. *J Learn Disabil*
2004 37: 466

Bryan G. Cook (2000). A comparison of teacher's attitudes towards their included
students with mild and severe disabilities. J Spec Educ January 2001 vol. 34 no. 4
203-213

Margolis, Leslie, Goodman, Susan (1999).Assistive Technology Services for Students: What Are These?Special Edition of Tech Express. 42-45

Neisser, U (1967). Cognitive psychology. Appleton-Century-Crofts: New York

Ted S. Hasselbring , Candyce H.Williams Glaser (2000). Use of Computer Technology to Help Students with Special Needs The Future of Children "Children and Computer Technology" Vol. 10, No. 2

Sandberg A, Granlund M(2004) Play experiences from childhood in adults with visual disability, motor disability and Asperger syndrome.Volume 6, Issue 2.